Teachings of Jesus

Level 2

EDITED BY J. WESLEY EBY

Beacon Hill Press of Kansas City
Kansas City, Missouri

CONTENTS

PRONUNCIATION GUIDE

Vowels

Symbol	Key Words	Usual Letters
ay	age, day	a, ai, ay
a	ask, cat	a
ah	father, ox	a, o
aw	auto, saw	a, au, aw
ee	each, see	e, ee, ea, ey, y
e	egg, bed	e
air	pair, bear	air, are, ear
er	her, bird	er, ir, ur
ie	ice, pie	i, ie, y
i	inch, sit	i
oh	oat, no	o, oa, oe, ow
ew	new, moon	u, ew, oo, ue
oo	good, bush	oo, u
ou	out, cow	ou, ow
oy	oil, boy	oi, oy
yew	use, human	u
u*	up, just (final or only sound of a syllable)	u
uh*	mother, ago (First or middle sound of a word or syllable)	any vowel

Consonants

Symbol	Key Words	Usual Letters
b	boat, cab	b, bb
ch	church, match	ch, tch
d	day, dad	d, dd
f	foot, wife	f, ff, ph, gh
g	gate, big	g, gg
h	hand, behind	h, wh
j	joy, page	j, g, dg
k	king, music	k, c, ck, ch
ks	box, sacks	x, cks
kw	queen, equal	qu
l	life, hill	l, ll
m	man, ham	m, mm
n	new, son	n, nn, kn
ng	drink, sing	n, ng
p	pig, cap	p, pp
r	race, year	r, rr, wr
s	sun, face	s, c, ss, sc
sh	sheep, fish	sh, ti
t	teach, mat	t, tt
th	thin, bath	th
th	this, bathe	th
v	vine, love	v
w	win, away	w
y	you, beyond	y
z	zeal, bees	z, zz, s
zh	measure	s, z

*This is the same as the schwa sound found in many dictionaries.

INTRODUCTION

You, the learner, will study the Bible in this book. The Bible is the words of God to us. We call it God's Word.

These lessons will help you learn about the Christian faith. You will study some of the teachings of Jesus Christ. You will learn some of the important things that Jesus taught. These lessons can help you become a Christian. If you are a Christian, these lessons can help you become a better Christian.

These lessons are for people who are learning English. They are also for people who are just learning to read English. These lessons will be helpful to people who are beginning to learn about the Bible. The writers want you to understand the Bible. They want you to understand the lessons. So, the sentences are not very long. Most of the words are words that you know. Or, the words will be easy for you to learn.

Your teacher will help you learn. Your teacher wants you to know about God and the Bible. So, do not be afraid to ask for help. Ask about the things you do not know or understand.

God loves you very much. He wants to be your God. He wants you to learn about Him. He wants you to believe in Jesus Christ. He wants Jesus to be your Savior.

You can pray and ask God to help you learn. He will help you know about Him. God will help you to believe His Word. Then, you will know God in your mind and in your heart.

—Editor

1 JESUS USED PARABLES IN TEACHING

Memory Verse: "Jesus answered, 'My *teaching* is not My own. It comes from Him [God] who sent Me.'" (John 7:16)
Scripture Lesson: Matthew 13:10-17, 51-52

Jesus was a great teacher. He taught the people when He lived on earth. He often used stories as He taught. The stories were about people and animals. The stories were about the people's everyday lives. These stories are called **parables**.

In this book, we will study some of the **teachings** of Jesus. We will study some of His parables. We can learn some important lessons from Jesus' teachings.

A. JESUS USED PARABLES TO HELP PEOPLE UNDERSTAND THE **KINGDOM OF HEAVEN**. (Matthew 13:10-17)

One day, Jesus' **disciples** came to Him. They asked Him why He used parables. Jesus said that parables are to help people understand the kingdom of heaven. He said that some people would understand the parables. Yet, some people would not understand the parables. Jesus reminded the disciples of what Isaiah (ie-ZAY-uh) said. Isaiah was a **prophet** in the Old Testament. Isaiah said that people would hear and see. But some people would not understand.

Jesus knew that people enjoyed stories. He knew that people remembered stories. They remembered stories about their everyday lives. He knew that people could understand the lessons in stories.

Today, we understand stories about our everyday lives. We understand a story about a hungry child if we have been hungry. We understand a story about **planting seeds** if we have planted seeds.

Today, we enjoy stories too. And we usually remember stories. Stories can help us learn what to do. Stories can also help us learn what we should not do. The parables in the Bible can help us learn the teachings of Jesus.

B. JESUS USED PARABLES TO **TRAIN** HIS DISCIPLES. (Matthew 13:51)

Jesus trained His disciples to be teachers, also. He wanted them to teach other people. He wanted them to know about God. He wanted them to understand His teachings. Jesus used parables to help His disciples understand what He taught.

Jesus knew the disciples would be better teachers if they understood His teachings. The disciples also knew that Jesus would **explain** the parables to them. Jesus often explained what the disciples did not understand. They were not afraid to ask Jesus what they did not understand.

Today, we learn about God and His Son, Jesus, in church. Your teacher wants you to know about God and Jesus. You should ask your teacher about the things you do not understand. Your teacher will be happy to help you. Your teacher will explain the things you do not know.

C. JESUS WANTED HIS DISCIPLES TO **SHARE** HIS TEACHINGS. (Matthew 13:52)

Jesus said that every teacher is like a person who owns a house. The owner of the house does not hide the things that he owns. The owner has things in his house for people to see and use. He has both new and old things. Some things are **treasures**. They are special to the owner. But, he does not keep the treasures just for himself. He shares them with other people.

Jesus said that a teacher will share what he has learned. A teacher will share what he knows. He will share new things and old things. He will teach from the New Testament. And he will teach from the Old Testament. The Bible is full of special treasures from God. The teacher will share these treasures with others.

Today, we can be like the disciples of Jesus. We can learn from our teachers. They help us learn about God and Jesus. They help us learn what the Word of God says. The things we learn are treasures. Then, we can share what we know with other people.

CONCLUSION

Jesus taught His disciples many things. He often used parables when He taught. The parables helped people to understand His teachings. The parables helped them to understand the kingdom of heaven.

Today, we can learn from our teachers. They will help us learn about God and Jesus. We can ask them about the things we do not know. Then, we need to share with other people what we learn. The Word of God is a special treasure. We need to share this treasure with others.

QUESTIONS: *Fill in the blanks.*

1. Jesus often used stories or _____ as He taught.
2. Jesus used parables to help people understand the
   _____ _____ _____.
3. Jesus knew His disciples could understand the
   _____ in the stories.
4. Today, people _____ stories and usually
   _____ them.
5. Jesus also used parables to _____ His disciples.
6. Jesus _____ to the disciples what they did not
   understand.
7. Jesus wanted His disciples to _____ His teachings
   with others.
8. The Bible is full of special _____ from God.

Here are some questions for you to think about and discuss:

1. Can you think of a story or parable that has helped you? How did
   the parable help you change something in your life?
2. Do you always understand the Bible or your lessons? What can
   you do to help you understand better?
3. How can you share Jesus' teachings with others?
4. Do you know of a "treasure" in the Bible? What is it? Would you
   share it with your teacher or a friend?

VOCABULARY:

1. **parables** (*noun*): short stories about everyday life that teach
   important lessons; (Jesus often used parables when He taught
   His disciples and other people.)
2. **teaching, teachings** (*noun*): what is taught; what a teacher
   helps other people to learn
3. **kingdom of heaven** (*noun phrase*): the kingdom of God; (The
   kingdom of heaven includes all people who believe and obey
   God. The kingdom of heaven is not the same as heaven.)
4. **disciples** (*noun*): the 12 men who followed Jesus here on earth
   and helped Jesus in His work
5. **prophet** (*noun*): a person who speaks for God; (A prophet gives
   a message from God to people.)

6. **planting seeds** (*verb phrase*): putting seeds in the ground so they will grow
7. **train** (*verb*): tell and show someone else how to do something; help people learn to do certain things
8. **explain** (*verb*): tell what something means; teach; tell all about something so other people will know about it too
9. **share** (*verb*): give away; give some of what you have to other people; tell what you know to other people
10. **treasures** (*noun*): things people own and love very much; things people own that are very important to them [people]

2 JESUS TAUGHT ABOUT GOD'S LOVE

Memory Verse: "For this son of mine . . . was lost and is found. . . ."
   (Luke 15:24)
Scripture Lesson: Luke 15:11-24

One day, Jesus told three parables. These stories were about things that were lost. The three lost things were a sheep, a coin, and a son. In each story, the lost thing was found. The parables teach us about the joy there is when lost things are found.

Today, we will study the parable of the lost son. The father is the most important person in the story. The father's love for his son is like God's love for us.

A. THE FATHER LETS THE SON LEAVE HOME. (Luke 15:11-16)

We need to know about the laws of the Jews to understand the story. The law said that children should honor and obey their parents. The law also told how the father's land and **wealth** would be **divided** when a father died. It told how much to give to each child.

In the parable, the father had two sons. One son asked for his part of his father's wealth before the father died. The son did not honor his father. The son did not obey the law.

The father could have punished the son. But, he did not. The father loved his son very much. He knew that he could not make the son love him. So, the father let the son leave home. The father gave the son his part of the wealth. He gave his son **freedom**.

The father waited for the son to return home. He was very sad. The father could not make the son return. The son had decided to leave home. Therefore, the son must decide to come home again.

B. THE SON RETURNED HOME. (Luke 15:17-20)

The son did not use his freedom wisely. He spent all his money. He was hungry and sad. Finally, he **decided** to go back home.

The son knew he had spent all his money. He knew the father might be angry with him. He knew his father might punish him. But he went home anyway. The son decided to ask his father to forgive him.

10

There was something that the son did not know. The father had forgiven him already. The father was waiting for the son to return home. He was waiting for the son to ask for **forgiveness**.

The father ran to meet his son. The father did not follow the **custom** of the country. The custom was that older men waited for people to come to them. But the father was too happy to wait. The father loved his son too much to wait.

The son asked the father to forgive him. He said that he had sinned against his father. The son knew he had no right to be called a son anymore.

C. THE FAMILY **CELEBRATED**. (Luke 15:21-24)

The father gladly forgave his son. He did not punish the young man. Instead, the father celebrated his son's return.

The father gave his son a robe, a ring, and shoes. These were special gifts. The robe showed that the father loved and honored the son. The ring showed that the son was an important part of the family. The shoes showed that the son was a free man.

The father had a party for his son. A fat calf was killed and cooked. Other special food was cooked. The people celebrated because the lost son came back home. The father said, "For this son of mine . . . was lost and is found. . . . ." (Luke 15:42)

CONCLUSION

This story is like the story of our lives. We are like the lost son who left his father. We leave our Father when we sin against Him. God is like the father. God is waiting for us to return to Him because He loves us.

The father was very sad when the son left home. But the father was very happy when the son returned. The father had great joy. He celebrated the son's return. God is also sad if we leave Him. God is sad when we sin and do not obey Him. But God is very happy when we return to Him. There is great joy in heaven when a sinner comes to God.

The father forgave the son. The son asked for forgiveness. The father gave gifts to his son. He loved his son very much. God forgives us when we ask for forgiveness. God also gives many gifts to his children. God loves us very much. He loves us because we are His children.

QUESTIONS: *Give the answers.*

1. How many sons did the father have? _____

2. What did one son ask for? His _____ of the father's
   _____.

3. Why was the son not wise? Because he spent _____
   _____ _____.

4. What did the son decide to do? _____
   _____.

5. What did the father gladly do for his son? _____
   _____.

6. Who is like the lost son in the story? _____

7. When will God forgive us? When we _____
   _____.

8. Why does God forgive us? Because He _____
   _____.

Here are some questions for you to think about and discuss:

1. Have you ever lost anything? How did you feel?

2. Have you ever left God? If so, why did you leave Him?

3. Why does God forgive sinners?

4. Do you need to ask God to forgive you? Are you willing to ask Him now?

VOCABULARY:

1. **wealth** (*noun*): riches and much money; all that a person owns

2. **divided** (*verb*): made into two or more parts

3. **freedom** (*noun*): the right to do what a person wants to do

4. **decided** (*verb*): chose; made a choice after thinking about it

5. **forgiveness** (*noun*): the act of forgiving someone; the act of God when he makes a person free from the guilt of sin

6. **custom** (*noun*): a habit; something people do as a part of their way of living

7. **celebrated** (*verb*): took part in a special time of joy; (Today, "celebrated" often is used in talking about parties and happy times, such as holidays.)

3 JESUS TAUGHT ABOUT LISTENING

Memory Verse: "He who has ears, let him hear." (Matthew 13:9)
Scripture Lesson: Matthew 13:3-9,18-23

One day, Jesus was teaching beside a lake. The crowd got bigger and bigger. The crowd was all around Jesus. He got into a boat and sat down. The people listened as Jesus taught them.

There were different types of people in the crowd. Jesus told the people a parable. The parable had different parts. There was a different part of the story for the different types of people.

A. THE PERSON WHO PLANTS SEEDS IS VERY IMPORTANT. (Matthew 13:3)

The parable was about a farmer who planted seeds. The story also told what happened to the seeds. A farmer is very important. He plants seeds in the ground. Plants cannot grow until the farmer puts the seeds in the ground.

Christians are like farmers. The Word of God is like the seeds. Christians should **plant the Word of God** like a farmer plants seeds. We should tell other people that Jesus loves them. We should tell other people how to become Christians.

B. THE TYPE OF SOIL IS IMPORTANT. (Matthew 13:4-8,18-23)

Jesus told about four types of soil. Jesus explained to His disciples what the story meant. The four types of soil are like the types of people who listened to Jesus. The seeds are like the words of Jesus.

The first type of soil is beside the garden. This soil is very hard. The seeds cannot get into the soil. The seeds stay on the top of the ground. Then birds come and eat the seeds.

Some people are like this soil. They do not want to hear the words of Jesus. These people do not try to understand Jesus teachings. Their minds and hearts are like the hard soil. Then the **devil** comes and takes away the Word of God from them.

The second type of soil is rocky soil. The soil may look good, but it is not. It is full of rocks under the top of the ground. The seeds start to grow. But, their roots soon hit the rocks. Their roots cannot go down into the soil. The plants cannot get water. So, the plants die.

Some people are like rocky soil. These people believe in Jesus. They are happy as Christians. But, they have problems. They may lose their jobs. Their children may become sick. Their friends may stop being their friends. Then, they do not use their faith in Jesus. Their faith in Jesus dies.

The third type of soil has thorns and weeds. The seeds start to grow. But, the thorns and weeds **choke** the young plants. The plants cannot get the food they need to grow. So, the small, new plants die.

Some people are like this type of soil. These people believe in Jesus. They work for Jesus. They try to do good things. But sometimes, they get too busy. They do not take time to pray and read the Bible. They think more about the things of life. They love money and what money can buy. They do not get the **spiritual** food they need. The things of life choke them. Soon, they die spiritual deaths.

The fourth type of soil is the good soil. It is not hard or rocky. There are no thorns or weeds. So, the plants grow. The farmer has a good **harvest**. He has a good crop.

Some people are like this type of soil. They listen to what Jesus says. They believe in Him and obey His teachings. They pray and read the Bible. They help other people believe in Jesus. They help people become a part of the kingdom of heaven. They have a good harvest of people for God.

C. JESUS TAUGHT THAT WE SHOULD BE GOOD **LISTENERS**. (Matthew 13:9)

Jesus said, "He who has ears, let him hear." (verse 9) Jesus meant that we must listen to and obey Him. We must decide which type of person we are. No one can decide for us. We must decide for ourselves. We should ask God to help us be like the good soil.

We should be a good listener all the time. We should listen to our pastor. We should listen to our Sunday School teacher. We should listen as we read the Bible. We should listen with both our ears and our hearts.

CONCLUSION

Jesus taught us about listening. It is not always easy to be a good listener. We must learn to be a good listener. We must ask Jesus to help us understand what we hear. We must ask Him to help us obey what we hear. Then, the Word of God will grow in the good soil of our lives.

QUESTIONS: *Fill in the blanks.*

1. _____ are like farmers. The
   _____ is like the seeds.

2. Christians should _____
   _____ like a farmer plants seeds.

3. Jesus told about _____ types of _____.

4. Some people are like hard soil. The _____ comes
   and takes away the _____ _____ _____.

5. Some people are like rocky soil. They believe in _____.
   But, when they have _____, their
   _____ in Jesus dies.

6. Some people are like soil with weeds. The things of life
   _____ them, and they die _____
   deaths.

7. Some people are like good soil. They have a good _____
   _____ _____ for God.

8. Jesus taught us to be good _____. He meant we
   must listen to and _____ Him.

Here are some questions for you to think about and discuss:

1. What kind of soil are you?
2. How can a person die a spiritual death?
3. How can a Christian have a harvest of people for God?
4. How can you be a good listener?
5. How do people listen with their "hearts"?

VOCABULARY:

1. **plant the Word of God** (*verb phrase*): tell other people what the Bible says; try to help people understand the teachings of Jesus
2. **devil** (*noun*): Satan; the enemy of God; the most powerful of evil spirits
3. **choke** (*verb*): cause something to stop growing

16

4. **spiritual** (*adjective*): describes something of the Spirit of God or Holy Spirit

5. **harvest** (*noun*): a crop of food that is ready to eat; (A harvest of people is everyone who believes in God and receives Jesus as Savior.)

6. **listeners** (*noun*): people who hear what is said; people who listen, understand, and obey the teachings of Jesus

4 JESUS TAUGHT ABOUT MONEY

Memory Verse: "You cannot serve both God and Money." (Luke 16:13)

Scripture Lesson: Luke 16:1-13

God cares about our use of money. There are more than 2,000 verses about money in the Bible. One of every 10 verses in the **Gospels** is about money. There are 38 parables in the Gospels. There are 16 of these parables about the use of money. In this lesson, we will study one of the parables about money.

A. GOD LETS PEOPLE BE **MANAGERS** OF MONEY. (Luke 16:1-2)

Jesus told a story about a rich man. The man had great wealth. He may have been a farmer with much land. So the rich man **hired** a person to help him. This person was called a manager.

The rich man heard that the manager was **cheating** him. The manager was not honest. He was not wise in the way he used the rich man's money. So the rich man **fired** the manager. The manager was fired because he was not honest.

God is the owner of all things. Today, God lets us be managers of what He gives us. God wants us to be wise with everything we own. He wants us to be honest.

B. GOOD MANAGERS PLAN CAREFULLY AND WISELY. (Luke 16:3-9)

The manager knew he would need help when he was fired. He would need food and a place to live. The manager had a plan. He would get the rich man's **debtors** to help him.

The debtors owed money to the rich man. The manager told his plan to the debtors. The debtors did not have to pay all their debts. They could pay the rich man less money than their debts. The debtors liked the plan. The manager knew the debtors would thank him by helping him. When he was fired, the debtors would give him food and a place to live. The manager was smart.

The rich man heard about the manager's plan. He told the manager that his plan was good. He knew that the manager was smart. The manager was wise to think about his future. He was wise to make plans. But, the rich man did not hire the manager again. The manager was not honest and could not be **trusted**.

We can learn a lesson from the manager. We need to think about our future. We need to plan carefully. God wants His children to plan carefully. He wants us to use our money wisely. But, He does not want us to cheat. He wants us to be honest. God says that we are not to steal. (Exodus 20:15)

C. GOOD MANAGERS CAN BE TRUSTED. (Luke 16:10-12)

The manager in this parable was not a good manager. He was **dishonest**. He could not be trusted.

Jesus told us how to be good managers. We must be **trustworthy** with what we have. We may have only a little money. We may have only a small job. But, can God trust us with the money we have? Can He trust us with doing a small job well? People who are trustworthy with very little will also be trustworthy with much. People who are dishonest with very little will also be dishonest with much.

D. GOOD MANAGERS USE THEIR MONEY WISELY. (Luke 16:13)

Some people use their money for evil. They use their money only for themselves. They buy things that hurt themselves or other people. They may be dishonest and cheat others. Money becomes a god to them. Money becomes their **master**.

Some people think that money is bad. But money is not bad or evil. Everyone needs money to live. Money used in right ways is good. We can use money to buy what we need. We can share our money with other people. And we can use money for God's work. If we use money wisely, we are good managers.

Jesus said, ". . . You cannot serve both God and Money." (verse 13) This means that we must choose between God and money. If we choose God, He is our Master. But if we choose money, it becomes our master and god. We must decide what is most important in our lives. Is it God? Or is it money?

CONCLUSION

We should be good managers of our money. We can learn to use our money wisely. We can use our money for the things we need. We can share our money with other people and with God. We can be masters of everything we have.

We should be trustworthy. We need to be trusted if we have little or if we have much. We need to be trusted with our money. We need to be trustworthy in our jobs. We need to be trustworthy all the time.

QUESTIONS: *Fill in the blanks.*

1. How many parables are in the Gospels? _____
   How many parables are about money? _____

2. Why did the rich man fire the manager? Because the manager
   _____.

3. Who is owner of all things? _____

4. What lesson can we learn from the manager? We need to
   _____.

5. How can we be good managers? We must be
   _____.

6. How can money be used for evil? When people
   _____.

7. How can money be used in the right way? When people use
   money _____.

8. What are we if we use money wisely? _____
   _____.

Here are some questions for you to think about and discuss:

1. How can you be a good manager?
2. Why is it important to be trustworthy? In what part of your life should you be trustworthy?
3. How can money be a god to people?
4. How can Christians use their money wisely?

VOCABULARY:

1. **Gospels** (*proper noun*): the first four books of the New Testament: Matthew, Mark, Luke, and John; (The Gospels tell about the life of Jesus Christ.)

2. **managers** (*noun*): people who take care of things that someone else owns
3. **hired** (*verb*): gave a job to someone; asked a person to work and gave them money for their work
4. **cheating** (*verb*): taking something by not being honest; stealing by tricking another person
5. **fired** (*verb*): took a job away from someone; (People are fired when they are no longer wanted or needed for work.)
6. **debtors** (*noun*): people who owe something to other people
7. **trusted** (*adjective*): believed in; (Trusted describes a person who always does what must be done or is asked to do.)
8. **dishonest** (*adjective*): not honest; not trustworthy
9. **trustworthy** (*adjective*): can be trusted; will always do what should be done or is asked to do
10. **master** (*noun*): owner; someone or something that has power over people

5 JESUS TAUGHT ABOUT REWARDS

Memory Verse: ". . . the Lord will reward everyone for whatever good he does . . ." (Ephesians 6:8)
Scripture Lesson: Matthew 20:1-16

The disciples followed Jesus. They left their jobs to go with Jesus. They left their families. They left everything to follow Him.

One day, a young man came to see Jesus. He had great wealth. The man asked Jesus how to have **eternal life**. Jesus told him to sell everything that he owned. Jesus said to give the money to poor people. The man was sad. He loved his wealth. He did not do what Jesus said. He did not receive eternal life.

The disciples saw the man leave. They had done what Jesus said to do. Peter reminded Jesus, "We have left everything to follow you! What then will there be for us?" (Matthew 19:27) The disciples thought they were better than the rich, young man. They thought God loved them more than He loved the man. They wanted to know what their **reward** would be. Would they have eternal life?

Jesus answered Peter by telling a parable. In this lesson, we will study the parable of the workers and the **vineyard**.

A. GOD ASKS US TO WORK FOR HIM. (Matthew 20:1-7)

Jesus told a story about a rich **landowner**. He had a large vineyard. The vineyard was a grape farm. The landowner needed some people to work in his vineyard. So the landowner went to town to hire some workers. These workers were poor. They did not have a job everyday. They were hired each day to do work.

The landowner told the first people that he hired how much he would pay them. A little later, he hired some more workers. But he did not tell them how much he would pay. He said that he would pay whatever was right. Several more times during the day, he hired workers for his vineyard. These workers had to trust the landowner for their pay.

Today, God needs many workers. He needs all of us. He has a job for every person. Our jobs may be big. Our jobs may be small. We need to trust God for our pay. He will reward us for the work we do.

B. GOD ASKS US TO BE **FAITHFUL** IN OUR JOBS.
(Matthew 20:8-12)

In the parable, the landowner gave all the workers the same pay. Some people worked for only one hour. These workers were not hired until late in the day. But these people worked well. They were faithful. So the landowner paid them for a day's work.

Some of the workers were angry. They had worked all day. They were faithful. They thought they **deserved** more money. They thought they were better than the other workers. But the landowner thought all the workers were the same. All of them were faithful. They did what the landowner hired them to do. So they all received the same reward.

Today, some people think that they are better than other people. They think that they are doing more for God. They think that their work is more important. They think that they deserve a greater reward from God.

God only asks that we be faithful. He wants us to be faithful with the jobs He has given us. No job is more important than another one. God just wants us to do our very best. He will reward us for being faithful.

C. GOD REWARDS US WHEN WE WORK FOR HIM.
(Matthew 20:13-16)

The workers who worked all day were not happy. They wanted more pay. But the landowner reminded them that they knew what pay they would receive. He did not owe them more money. He said that he could do what he wanted with his money.

Today, God will reward us for our work for Him. He will be faithful to reward us. But God does not have to pay us. He does not owe us anything. Yet, God gave His only Son to die for our sins. We can never deserve His love.

God does not want us to work because we will get a reward. He wants us to work because we love people. God wants us to work for Him because we love Him.

Jesus said, "So the last will be first, and the first will be last." (verse 16) He meant that we should not think we are better than anyone else. People, who think they are better, think they should have first place. But Jesus said these people will be last. Their reward will be the last place.

CONCLUSION

God has a job for every person. The job may be big or small. Yet the job will be right for us. God wants us to be faithful. He wants us to be faithful in our jobs. Then, God will reward us. And He will be just and right in His rewards.

QUESTIONS: *Fill in the blanks.*

1. In this parable, there was a rich _____ who had a large _____.
2. The landowner _____ many people to work in the vineyard.
3. God needs many _____. He has a _____ for every person.
4. Some workers thought they _____ more money because they had _____ all day.
5. God only asks that we be _____ in our work.
6. God does not _____ us anything. Yet, He gave His only _____ to _____ for our _____.
7. God wants us to work for Him because _____ _____.
8. The memory verse says, ". . . the _____ will _____ everyone for whatever _____ he does . . ." (_____ 6: _____)

Here are some questions for you to think about and discuss:

1. How can people receive eternal life? Do you have eternal life?
2. What are some ways you can work for God? Has God given you a job to do?
3. How can you be faithful in working for God?
4. How does God reward us for working for Him?

VOCABULARY:

1. **eternal life** (*noun phrase*): life that has no end; life as a child of God on earth and living with God in heaven forever

24

2. **rewards** (*noun*): money or things you receive for doing something well; what you receive for doing something that is not a part of your job; special pay for doing a job

   reward (verb): to pay someone for doing a job

3. **vineyard** (*noun*): a garden or farm of grape plants or vines; a place where a farmer grows grapes

4. **landowner** (*noun*): a person who owns land; (In this lesson, the landowner was a farmer of grapes.)

5. **faithful** (*adjective*): trustworthy; can be trusted; true to God; always does what should be done

6. **deserved** (*verb*): earned; should be paid; were good enough for

6 JESUS TAUGHT ABOUT BEING GOOD NEIGHBORS

Memory Verse: ". . . Love your neighbor as yourself." (Luke 10:27)
Scripture Lesson: Luke 10:25-37

We need to know two things to help us understand this lesson. First, the Jews and **Samaritans** (suh-MAIR-uh-tunz) hated each other. The Samaritans lived near the Jews. The Jews and Samaritans would not talk to each other. Often, the Jews would not travel through the country of Samaria (suh-MAIR-ee-uh). They would go around Samaria even though the trip was longer.

Second, a man talked to Jesus and tried to **trick** Him. This man studied the laws of the Jews. He was a teacher of the law. He believed the laws were very important. This man wanted to see if Jesus knew the laws. He asked Jesus, "What must I do to [receive] eternal life?" (verse 25)

Jesus knew that the man wanted to trick Him. So, Jesus asked the man, "What is written in the Law?" (verse 26) The man answered Jesus' question. Then he asked Jesus, "And who is my **neighbor**?" (verse 29) Jesus answered the question by telling a parable. In this lesson, we will study the parable of the good Samaritan.

A. WE MUST LOVE GOD AND OUR NEIGHBOR. (Luke 10:25-29)

The law said that we must love God. We must love Him with all our heart, soul, strength, and mind. We must love God more than anyone or anything. God must be first in our lives.

The law also said that we must love our neighbors. We must love our neighbors as we love ourselves. God made all people. Every person is important to God. Therefore, every person should be important to us.

The man who came to Jesus knew the law. He told Jesus what the law said. Then he asked, "Who is my neighbor?" Jesus answered him with a story.

B. WE MUST DECIDE TO LOVE OUR NEIGHBOR. (Luke 10:30-37)

One day, a Jew was on a trip. He was going from the city of Jerusalem (Juh-REW-suh-lum) to the city of Jericho (JAIR-uh-coh).

Some robbers beat the man. They took his clothes and money. They left him beside the road to die.

A **priest** walked by the man. He was a Jew, but he walked by on the other side of the road. He did not stop and help the man who was hurt. Next, a **Levite** (LEE-viet) walked by the man. The Levite was a Jew also. He walked near the man, but he also did not stop and help him.

Then, a Samaritan walked by the man. Samaritans hated the Jews. And the Jews hated them. But, this Samaritan felt sorry for the Jew. He stopped to help the man. He cared for his cuts. He took him to an **inn**. He gave money to the owner of the inn to care for the man.

Jesus then asked the teacher of the law a question: "Which of these three men was a neighbor to the man who was robbed?" The teacher answered, "The one who helped him." Jesus said, "Go and do the same."

Today, many people are like the priest and Levite. They say that they love God. They say that they obey God. But they do not show love to other people. Their **actions** do not agree with their words. They do not love their neighbors.

Some people are like the good Samaritan. They see people with needs. They take time to help other people. Their actions show love. They are good neighbors.

Sometimes, it is not easy to help our neighbors. It may take some of our time. It may take some of our money. Our neighbors may not be people we like. Our neighbors may hate us. The devil may try to trick us. The devil does not want us to obey Jesus. But, we should remember the words of Jesus, "Go and do the same." We should show our neighbors Christian love. Our actions should show them the love of Jesus.

The Bible does not tell us what the teacher of the law did. We do not know if he obeyed Jesus. We do not know if he decided to be a good neighbor. But today, we can decide what type of neighbors we are. We can decide to be like the priest and Levite. Or, we can decide to be like the Samaritan. We can decide to love our neighbors as we love ourselves.

CONCLUSION

Jesus taught us what good neighbors are. Good neighbors love all people. They love people who have needs. They help people who need help. They show Jesus' love by their actions. They obey Jesus' teaching to love their neighbors.

QUESTIONS: *Fill in the blanks.*

1. Whom does the law say we must love? _____ and

   _____ _____

2. Where was a Jew going? From _____ to

   _____.

3. What happened to the Jew? _____

   _____.

4. Who did not help the man who was robbed? A

   _____ and a _____.

5. Who helped the man who was robbed? A _____

   _____.

6. Who was a neighbor to the man who was robbed? _____

   _____

7. What should we show to our neighbors? _____

   _____

8. What did Jesus do for us? He _____

   _____.

Here are some questions for you to think about and discuss:

1. Were the priest and Levite good neighbors? Why or why not?
2. Why was the Samaritan a good neighbor?
3. Who are our neighbors? How can we be good neighbors today?
4. Is there someone you do not love? How can you learn to love that person?

VOCABULARY:

1. **Samaritans** (*proper noun*): people who lived in the country of Samaria; (Samaritans lived near the Jews. The Jews and Samaritans were neighbors but they hated each other.)
2. **trick** (*verb*): to fool; not be honest with

3. **neighbors** (*noun*): people who live near each other; (In this lesson, neighbors include all people on earth.)
4. **priest** (*noun*): a religious or church leader of the Jews; a man who gave messages from God to the people
5. **Levite** (*proper noun*): a person in the family of priests for the Jews; a religious or church leader of the Jews
6. **inn** (*noun*): a place to stay at night for people who travel; a motel or hotel
7. **actions** (*noun*): deeds; acts; the things people do

7 JESUS TAUGHT ABOUT PRAYER

Memory Verse: ". . . Ask and it will be given to you; seek and you will find; knock and the door will be opened to you." (Luke 11:9)
Scripture Lesson: Luke 11:1-13

One day, Jesus prayed to God. The disciples wanted to know how to pray, too. One of the disciples said, "Lord, teach us to pray." (verse 1) So Jesus did.

The prayer that Jesus taught is called the Lord's Prayer. You can read it in verses 2-4. The Lord's Prayer is also in Matthew 6:9-13. It is a good prayer to learn. It is a prayer that we can pray every day.

Jesus wanted to train His disciples to pray. He wanted them to know that prayer is important. After Jesus prayed, He told a parable. This story helps us to understand prayer better. We can learn some important lessons from Jesus' teachings about prayer.

A. GOD WANTS US TO **PERSIST** IN PRAYER. (Luke 11:5-8)

Jesus said that prayer is like **borrowing** some bread from a neighbor. One night, you have a friend come to your house. He is on a trip and comes to see you. But you do not have any food for him to eat. So you go to your neighbor to borrow three loaves of bread. You are **bold**.

You knock on the neighbor's door. But he answers, "Don't bother me." He says that he and the family are in bed. He says that he cannot get up to give you the bread.

Jesus said that the neighbor will finally get up. He will give you the loaves of bread. He will let you borrow the food if you persist. You need the food, so you persist. You knock and knock on the door. You ask and ask and ask. You do not stop asking until he gives you the bread. You get what you need because you are bold. You get what you need because you persist.

We can learn a lesson from this story. We should be bold when we pray. We should not be afraid to ask God for the things we need. We should persist in prayer. We should not stop praying. We should not stop asking God for what we need.

B. GOD WANTS US TO ASK HIM FOR OUR NEEDS. (Luke 11:9-10)

Jesus explained the parable. Jesus said to ask, **seek**, and knock when we pray. If you ask, you receive what you are asking for. If you seek, you find what you are looking for. If you knock, the door opens for you.

When we pray, we can ask God for what we need. God promises to give us what we need. Paul wrote to the church in Philippi (fuh-LIP-ie), "And my God will meet all your needs . . . in Christ Jesus." (Philippians 4:19) This is a treasure in the Word of God! This is a wonderful promise!

When we pray, we can seek to find **God's will.** Christians need to know what God's will is for their lives. We need to know that the things we ask for are His will. The Bible says, ". . . if we ask anything according to His will, He hears us." (1 John 5:14) Sometimes, we ask for things that are not God's will. We need to seek His will. And we need to pray according to His will. He knows what is best for us.

When we pray, we can knock on the door of the future. When a door is closed, we do not know what is on the other side. But when a door is open, then we know. In our lives, our futures are like the other side of a door. We do not know what our futures will be. But, we do not need to be afraid. God says, "For I know the plans I have for you . . . plans to give you hope and a future." (Jeremiah 29:11) We can knock on the door and God will open it for us. We can trust God with our futures.

C. GOD GIVES GOOD GIFTS TO HIS CHILDREN. (Luke 11:11-13)

Fathers give good gifts to their children. They do not give their children things that will hurt them. They love their children and want what is best for them. They even give gifts to children who do not deserve them.

God is our Father in heaven. He loves us very much. He loves us more than our own fathers love us. He does not trick us. He wants what is best for us. He gives us good gifts. He gives us gifts even though we do not deserve them.

Sometimes, we do not know what is best for our lives. We may ask our Father for things that we should not have. We may ask for things that are not for our good. But, God knows. We can trust Him to give us what is best. He is always trustworthy.

CONCLUSION

We can pray to God, our Father. He loves us very much. He wants us to pray to Him. He wants us to be bold in praying to Him. He wants us to persist in our prayers. He wants us to ask, seek, and knock. And He will give His children good gifts.

QUESTIONS: *Fill in the blanks.*

1. The prayer that Jesus taught His disciples is called _____
   _____ _____.

2. God wants us to _____ in prayer.

3. We should be _____ when we pray. We should not
   be _____ to ask God for things we need.

4. Jesus said to _____, _____, and
   _____ when we pray.

5. God promises to give us _____
   _____.

6. Christians can seek to find _____
   _____.

7. We can trust God with our _____.

8. God is our _____ in _____.
   He gives His children _____ _____.
   We can trust Him to give us what is _____.

Here are some questions for you to think about and discuss:

1. How can we be bold when we pray? How can we persist in prayer?

2. What has God given you that you asked Him for?

3. Why should we seek to find God's will?

4. Are you afraid of the future? How can you trust God with your future?

5. What good gifts have you received from God?

VOCABULARY:

1. **persist** (*verb*): not stop; not quit; not give up

2. **borrowing** (*verb*): asking to use something that another person owns; (You agree to return what you borrow.)
3. **bold** (*adjective*): not afraid; brave; have no fear
4. **seek** (*verb*): look for; ask for; try to find
5. **God's will** (*noun phrase*): what God wants for people

8 JESUS TAUGHT ABOUT BEING HUMBLE

Memory Verse: "... he who humbles himself will be exalted."
(Luke 14:11 and 18:14)
Scripture Lesson: Luke 14:7-11; 18:9-14

There are two parables in this lesson. These parables teach us about being **humble**. We can learn from these stories how Jesus wants us to live.

Jesus did not tell these stories at the same time. But both stories are about being humble. So, we will study them in the same lesson.

A. HUMBLE PEOPLE **RESPECT** OTHER PEOPLE. (Luke 14:7-10)

One day, Jesus was a guest for dinner at the house of a **Pharisee** (FAIR-uh-see). He watched the other guests as they chose where to sit. Jesus knew that the most important guests sat next to the **host**. Jesus watched the guests as they sat down. They wanted to sit in an important place. The guests wanted to show how important they were.

Jesus saw how the people acted. He did not like their actions. He did not want people to think they were important. He wanted them to be humble.

Jesus told the guests a story. He said that you may be invited to a dinner. But you should not sit in the most important place. Someone more important than you may also be invited. Then the host will have to tell you to sit in another place. You will be **ashamed** because the host had to tell you to move.

Jesus said that you should sit in the least important place. This will show that you respect other people. Later, the host may tell you to move to a more important place. You will be honored and not ashamed. Then the other guests will respect you.

Today, many people want to be important. They are not humble. They do not show respect to others. But, Jesus has not changed. He does not want us to think we are important. Jesus wants us to put other people first. A humble person thinks of other people. A humble person respects others.

B. HUMBLE PEOPLE ARE HONEST WITH THEMSELVES. (Luke 18:9-13)

Another day, Jesus was talking to some people. They thought they were good people. They thought that they were right with God. But they did not respect others. These people were not humble. So, Jesus told this story.

Two men went to the temple to pray. One was a Pharisee. The other man was a **tax collector**. The Pharisee prayed about himself. He told God how good he thought he was. He said, "God, I thank You that I am not like other men . . ." (verse 11) The Pharisee was not humble. He was not honest with himself.

The tax collector also prayed. He did not tell God how good he was. Instead, he said, "God, have **mercy** on me, a sinner." (verse 13) He knew that he had sinned against God. He knew that he did not deserve God's love. He knew that he needed God's mercy. He was humble. He was honest with himself.

Jesus said that the God forgave the tax collector. But God did not forgive the Pharisee. The Pharisee did not ask for mercy.

Today, we need to be humble. We need to be humble when we pray. We should not try to make people think we are important. And we cannot make God think we are important. He knows our thoughts and hearts. He knows if we are honest. Instead, we need to ask God for mercy.

C. HUMBLE PEOPLE WILL BE **EXALTED**. (Luke 14:11; 18:14)

The memory verse says, ". . . he who humbles himself will be exalted." Jesus said this at the end of each parable. Jesus meant that people who are humble will be honored. Humble people will be respected. Humble people will be exalted. But they will be exalted because others make them important. They will not be exalted because they think they are important.

Today, we should look at ourselves. Christians should look carefully at their thoughts. We should ask ourselves: "Do I think I am important? Do I think I am more important than I am? Am I a humble person?"

CONCLUSION

God wants us to be humble. And Jesus taught us to be humble. Sometimes, it may be difficult to be humble. The devil will try to make us think we are important. We need to pray and ask God to help us. We need to be like the tax collector. We need to ask God to have mercy on us. Then, we will be exalted.

————————————————————

QUESTIONS: *Give the answers.*

1. Who invited Jesus for dinner? _____

2. Why did Jesus not like the guests' actions? Because He
   _____.

3. What place did Jesus say to sit in? The _____
   _____ place.

4. Whom should we put first? _____
   _____

5. Who went to the temple to pray? A _____
   and a _____ _____.

6. Which man did God forgive? The _____
   _____.

7. Why was the tax collector humble? Because he did not tell God
   _____
   _____.

8. What will happen to people who humble themselves? They will
   be _____.

Here are some questions for you to think about and discuss:

1. How do some people act today to show that they are important?
2. How can a person be humble? Are you humble?
3. Why should a Christian be humble?
4. How can we show respect to other people?

————————————————————

VOCABULARY:

1. **humble** (*adjective*): describes people who do not think they are better than they are; not thinking of yourself as important
   humbles (*verb*): does not think of himself as important or better than other people

2. **respect** (*verb*): think well of a person; think of a person as important

3. **Pharisee** (*proper noun*): a religious leader of the Jews
4. **host** (*noun*): a person who takes care of guests in his home
5. **ashamed** (*adjective*): felt shame or guilt; felt bad because you made a mistake or did something wrong
6. **tax collector** (*noun phrase*): a person who gets tax money from people for a country or a government; (A tax collector in Jesus' time often cheated people and got rich. They were not liked or respected by other people.)
7. **mercy** (*noun*): help that is given to people who cannot help themselves; (God gives mercy to sinners when He forgives them. Sinners deserve to be punished for their sins.)
8. **exalted** (*adjective*): made important; honored; gave praise to

9 JESUS TAUGHT ABOUT DISCIPLESHIP

Memory Verse: "And anyone who does not carry his cross and follow Me cannot be My disciple." (Luke 14:27)

Scripture Lesson: Luke 14:25-30

Large crowds of people followed Jesus. They listened to Him. They heard His teachings. He told them what they must do to follow Him. He never tried to trick anyone into following Him. Jesus explained what He wanted the disciples to do. He said that being a disciple would not be easy.

In this lesson, we will study what Jesus wants His disciples to be. We will learn what **discipleship** means.

A. JESUS **DEMANDS** THAT WE LOVE HIM MORE THAN ANYONE ELSE. (Luke 14:25-26)

You may be surprised at what Jesus said. You may be surprised that Jesus said to hate anyone. We think of Jesus telling us to love all people.

We need to understand what "hate" means in this verse. The word "hate" in this verse comes from a special word. The word comes from the language used when Jesus was on earth. The word means "to love less." Jesus wants us to love our parents less than we love Him. He wants us to love our children less than we love Him. Jesus wants us to love Him more than anyone else.

Jesus does not hate families. He had special love for little children. He had special love for His own mother. He asked a friend to care for His mother when He died. Jesus tells us to call God "our Father." Thus, Jesus did not demand us to hate. Instead, He demanded us to love. We must decide to love Jesus more than we love our families.

B. JESUS DEMANDS THAT WE OBEY HIM EVERY DAY. (Luke 14:27)

God changes people when they become Christians. He changes their lives. He changes the way they think and what they do.

People who are not Christians may not understand these changes. Some people may not like these changes. Some people may not want to be our friends anymore. Some people may even be mean to us because we are Christians. A few people may hate us.

Jesus knows that these changes may be difficult for us. This is what He means to **carry a cross**. He does not mean a real cross to carry in our hands. But, He means that we must be willing to make changes for Him. We must be willing to do what He tells us to do. We must obey Him all the time. We must carry a cross and follow Him. We must do God's will. This is discipleship.

We must do more than go to church to be Jesus' disciple. We must do more than read the Bible and pray. We must do more than love our neighbors. We must follow Jesus and obey Him.

C. JESUS DEMANDS THAT WE PLAN CAREFULLY TO BE HIS DISCIPLE. (Luke 14:28-30)

Jesus wants us to understand how to be a good disciple. He told a parable about a **builder** and a **tower**.

The builder of a tower will look at his plans carefully. He will study the plans before building the tower. He will decide how much it will cost to build the tower. He will be certain that he has enough money. A good builder wants to start and finish the tower. If he does not plan well, he will not finish. People will not respect him.

Some towers or buildings may take a long time to build. A good **foundation** must be built first. Then the building is built upon the foundation. Then the building will be strong. Then the building will not fall down. It will not fall down because it has a strong foundation.

Jesus meant that we must decide what discipleship will cost. It may cost us our families. It may cost us our friends. It may cost us our jobs. Discipleship may cause many changes in our lives. So, we must plan carefully to be Jesus' disciples.

We should build a strong foundation for our Christian lives. We build a good foundation by reading the Bible and praying. We build a strong foundation by following and obeying Jesus. We build a strong foundation by carrying the cross of discipleship. A strong foundation will help us not to sin. Then we will not "fall down" as Christians. Then we can start and finish our Christian lives on earth.

CONCLUSION

Jesus taught us what we must do to be His disciples. We must love Him more than anyone else. We must obey Him all the time. We must plan carefully. Jesus knows that discipleship may be difficult. But He will help us. Jesus is trustworthy. He will help us to carry our cross and follow Him.

QUESTIONS: *Fill in the blanks.*

1. The word "hate" means _____ _____ _____ in Luke 14:26.

2. Jesus did not _____ us to hate. Instead, He demanded us to _____.

3. God _____ people when they become Christians. He changes the way they _____ and what they _____.

4. The memory verse says: "Anyone who does not _____ _____ _____ and _____ Me cannot be My _____."

5. "Carry a cross" means that we must be willing to make changes for _____. We must _____ Jesus all the time.

6. We build a strong foundation for our Christian lives by _____ and _____ Jesus.

7. Jesus demands three things to be His disciples. Write them. (Look at the sections A, B, and C.)

   (A) _____.
   (B) _____.
   (C) _____.

Here are some questions for you to think about and discuss:

1. Are you willing to be Jesus' disciple? How can you be His disciple?

2. God changes people who are Christians. Have you let God change you? How has God changed you?

3. Do you love Jesus more than your family and friends? How can you love Jesus more than anyone else?

4. What does "carry a cross" mean to you?

5. How can you build a strong foundation for your Christian life?

VOCABULARY:

1. **discipleship** (*noun*): being a disciple of Jesus; living the Christian life, obeying Jesus completely; doing God's will
2. **demands** (*verb*): commands; says we should
3. **carry his cross, carry a cross** (*verb phrase*): obey Jesus completely; do God's will; follow Jesus and do what He says
4. **builder** (*noun*): a person who builds
5. **tower** (*noun*): a tall building; a strong building
6. **foundation** (*noun*): the base upon which a building or tower is built; (A strong foundation is needed so the building or tower will not fall down.)

10 JESUS TAUGHT ABOUT THE KINGDOM OF GOD

Memory Verse: ". . . go and proclaim the kingdom of God." (Luke 9:60)

Scripture Lesson: Mark 4:26-32; 1 Corinthians 3:5-9

Jesus taught about the **kingdom of God** many times. He wanted the people to understand the kingdom of God. The kingdom of God was not easy to understand. So, Jesus told many parables to help the people understand. In this lesson, we will study two parables about seeds. Jesus **compared** the kingdom of God to seeds that grow.

A. THE KINGDOM OF GOD IS LIKE A GROWING SEED.
   (Mark 4:26-29)

Jesus said that the kingdom of God is like a farmer who plants seeds. The farmer plants wheat seeds in the ground. Then the seeds grow. The farmer does not know how they grow. Yet, the seeds grow and become a wheat crop. When the plants are ready to harvest, the farmer harvests the wheat. He then has food to eat and sell.

Jesus compared the seeds to the kingdom of God. We plant **spiritual seeds** when we tell people about Jesus. We plant spiritual seeds as we live for Jesus every day. We **proclaim** the kingdom of God by our words and our actions.

Then, these spiritual seeds grow in the hearts and lives of other people. We do not know how these seeds grow. But after a time, the seeds are ready to harvest. The people believe in Jesus as their Savior. They become Christians. The kingdom of God grows just like the seeds grow.

B. THE KINGDOM OF GOD IS LIKE A SMALL **MUSTARD** SEED.
   (Mark 4:30-32)

Jesus said the kingdom of God is like a mustard seed. The mustard seed is the smallest seed a farmer plants. Yet when it grows, it becomes the largest plant in the garden. It grows so large that birds can sit in it.

Jesus compared the kingdom of God to the mustard seed. The spiritual seeds we plant are like the mustard seeds. The "seeds" we plant may be very small. The "seed" may be a kind act. It may be a few kind words. It may be a smile. Yet, these seeds will grow in other people.

The small spiritual seeds that we plant help us proclaim Jesus Christ. These seeds grow in the hearts of other people. Then the kingdom of God grows as they become Christians. Then God's kingdom grows bigger and bigger and bigger. His kingdom is big enough for all people on earth. His kingdom is big enough for you.

C. GOD USES PEOPLE TO BUILD HIS KINGDOM.
   (1 Corinthians 3:5-9)

Paul wrote to the Christians in Corinth (KOHR-unth). Paul had been to Corinth and taught the people about God. Apollos (uh-PAHL-us) taught the people after Paul left Corinth.

Paul compared his teaching to planting seeds. He proclaimed Jesus Christ to the Corinthians. He planted spiritual seeds in their hearts. Paul compared the teaching of Apollos to watering seeds. Apollos taught and explained the Word of God. He did what he could to help the spiritual seeds grow.

Yet, Paul said that it was God who made the seeds grow. Paul and Apollos had important jobs. But their jobs were not the most important. Only God could make the spiritual seeds grow.

In the kingdom of God, every person has a job to do. Some people plant the seeds. They plant spiritual seeds by proclaiming Jesus Christ. Some people water the seeds. They teach and explain the Word of God to others. Some people take care of the plants. They love people and care for their everyday needs.

We will not harvest the crop of spiritual seeds. Only God can do that. But, we must be faithful. We must do the jobs that God tells us to do. Then, God will harvest the seeds. This means that God knows when a person is ready to become a Christian.

All of us are workers in the kingdom of God. We are like farmers who plant, water, and take care of seeds. Every person has an important job to do. Only God can make the seeds grow. Yet, God will reward us for our work. He will reward us because we are faithful. Then we will share in the harvest of people in God's kingdom.

CONCLUSION

The kingdom of God is growing. It grows as people believe in Jesus Christ. And God wants us to help in the kingdom. We can help plant spiritual seeds. Or we can help water the seeds. Or we can help take care of the plants. Each of us has a job to do. And God will reward us for our work.

QUESTIONS: *Give the answers.*

1. What did Jesus compare the kingdom of God to?

   _____

2. How do we plant spiritual seeds? When _____

   _____.

3. How do we proclaim the kingdom of God? By our

   _____ and _____.

4. Who proclaimed Jesus Christ to the Christians in Corinth?

   _____

5. Who taught and explained the Word of God to the Corinthians?

   _____

6. Who will harvest the crop of spiritual seeds? _____

7. Why will God reward us? Because _____

   _____.

8. Who are workers in the kingdom of God? _____

   _____

Here are some questions for you to think about and discuss:

1. The kingdom of God is big enough for every person. Are you a part of God's kingdom?
2. How can Christians proclaim the kingdom of God?
3. How can Christians plant spiritual seeds? How can you plant spiritual seeds?
4. What job or jobs do you have in the kingdom of God? Do you feel that your job is important?
5. How can you be faithful?

VOCABULARY:

1. **kingdom of God** (*noun phrase*): all the people who believe in

44

and receive Jesus as Savior, now and forever; (The kingdom of God is the same as the kingdom of heaven. See Lesson 1.)

2. **compared** (*verb*): showed through words how things are alike
3. **spiritual seeds** (*noun phrase*): words or actions that help other people know about God and His love
4. **proclaim** (*verb*): preach; teach; tell; share; (In this lesson, proclaim means to preach, teach, tell, or share the good news of Jesus.)
5. **mustard** (*noun*): a garden plant that is used in cooking food; (The mustard plant has a very small seed.)

11 JESUS TAUGHT ABOUT OBEDIENCE

Memory Verse: ". . . If anyone loves Me, he will obey My teaching . . . ." (John 14:23)
Scripture Lesson: Matthew 7:21-27

One day, Jesus went up on the side of a mountain. His disciples came to Him. Jesus taught them many things. We call these teachings the Sermon on the Mount. The Sermon on the Mount is in Matthew, chapters 5, 6, and 7.

There are many teachings in the Sermon on the Mount. Jesus wanted His disciples to learn these teachings. He wanted His disciples to obey Him. We will study a part of the Sermon on the Mount. We will study what Jesus said about **obedience**.

A. WE **ENTER** THE KINGDOM OF HEAVEN WHEN WE OBEY. (Matthew 7:21-23)

Jesus said that many people say they are Christians. But these people are not true Christians. They may go to church. They may be kind and help other people. They may know what the Bible says. They may know who Jesus is. Yet, they are not Christians. They are not a part of the kingdom of God.

Christians are people who believe that Jesus is the Son of God. Christians believe that Jesus died for their sins. They are sorry for their sins. They have asked God to forgive their sins. They have received Jesus into their hearts. Then, Christians enter the kingdom of heaven here on earth. Then, they follow Jesus Christ in obedience.

Jesus said that some people may **prophesy**. Some people may do **miracles**. These people may think that they are Christians because they prophesy. They may think that they are Christians because they do miracles. But, some people are not true Christians. These people have not believed in Jesus as their Savior. They know about Him. But they do not know Him.

Christians may prophesy. And Christians may do miracles. But these things do not make a person a Christian. Only the people who do God's will can enter God's kingdom. (verse 21) This means that they must obey God. They must obey the teachings of Jesus. They must live in obedience to God.

B. WE BUILD A STRONG FOUNDATION WHEN WE OBEY. (Matthew 7:24-27)

Jesus knew how to build things. He knew how to build houses. Jesus told a parable about builders at the end of the Sermon on the Mount. In the story, He compared builders and obedience to His teachings.

Jesus said that a person who obeys His teachings is like a wise builder. He built his house on the rock. This means that he built on a strong foundation. The foundation kept the house from falling down in the rain, flood, and wind. The house was safe in the storm. The house was safe on a strong foundation.

A person who does not obey Jesus' teachings is like a **foolish** builder. The foolish man built his house on the sand. The house did not have a strong foundation. The house fell down in the rain, flood, and wind. The house was not safe because it did not have a strong foundation.

Jesus said that we should be like the wise man. We should build on a strong foundation. But, He is not talking about building a house. Jesus is talking about the way we live our lives.

We should use the teachings of Jesus as our strong foundation. We should believe what He taught. And we should obey His teachings. Every time we obey Jesus our foundations becomes stronger.

The rain, flood, and wind have a special meaning. They mean the difficult times in our lives. They mean when we are sick or hurt. They mean the times people are not kind to us. They mean any problem we may have.

We should build our spiritual house with a strong foundation. Then we will be safe. We will be safe during the difficult times in our lives. God will take care of us. He will help us with all our problems.

The foolish man built a house without a foundation. He did not ask for help. The foolish man trusted in himself. He did not build wisely. So, his house fell down in the storm.

We must not be like the foolish man. We must not trust in ourselves. We must ask God for help. We must trust God to help us. Or, our spiritual house will fall down in the storms of life.

CONCLUSION

Jesus wants to be our Savior. He wants all of us to enter the kingdom of God. He wants us to do God's will. Jesus wants us to obey His teachings. He wants us to live in obedience to Him. Jesus said, ". . . If anyone love Me, he will obey My teaching . . . ." (John 14:23)

QUESTIONS: *Fill in the blanks.*

1. The name of Jesus' teachings in Matthew 5, 6, and 7 is called the

   _____ _____ _____

   _____.

2. Christians are people who believe that _____ is the Son of _____. They are _____ for their _____. They have asked God to _____ their sins. They have _____ Jesus into their hearts and _____.

3. Only people who do God's _____ can _____ the kingdom of God.

4. A person who obeys Jesus' teachings is like a _____ _____. He has built upon a _____ _____.

5. We should use the _____ of _____ to build a strong foundation.

6. We should build our _____ house with a strong foundation. Then we will be _____ in the storms of life.

7. The man was foolish because he _____ in himself.

8. We must be like the _____ man. We should not be like the _____ man.

Here are some questions for you to think about and discuss:

1. Are you a Christian? What must a person do to become a Christian?

2. What is meant by these sentences: "They know about Him [Jesus]. But they do not know Him."

3. What is meant by "building a spiritual house"?

4. How can we build on "strong foundations"?
5. What is meant by the storms of life? How has Jesus kept you safe in the storms of life?

VOCABULARY:

1. **obedience** (*noun*): the act of obeying; doing what someone demands or commands; doing what you know is right to do
2. **enter** (*verb*): go or come into; become a part of
3. **prophesy** (*noun*): preach; proclaim the Word of God; give a message from God to people; tell what will happen in the future
4. **miracles** (*noun*): things that only God can do; (Miracles show the great power of God.)
5. **foolish** (*adjective*): not wise; (Foolish describes a person who does something without careful and wise planning.)

12 Jesus Taught About Planning for Eternity

Memory Verse: "For where your treasure is, there your heart will be also." (Matthew 6:21)

Scripture Lesson: Luke 12:13-21; Matthew 6:19-21

Every person needs some money. We need money to buy the things we need to live. Yet, many people think that they do not have enough money. They think that they will be happy if they have wealth. They think that they will be happy if they can buy many things.

Sometimes, people want more than they own. They want more and more things. But, Jesus said that this is **greed**. And greed is wrong. Greed is a sin. We will study about greed in this lesson. We will also study about planning for **eternity**.

A. JESUS SAID THAT WE SHOULD NOT BE GREEDY.
     (Luke 12:13-15)

One day, Jesus was teaching a crowd of people. A man asked Jesus to do something. The man wanted his brother to divide some money with him. The man wanted Jesus to demand the brother to divide the money. The man thought that he deserved the money. But, Jesus knew that this was a family **argument**. And He did not want to be part of a family argument.

Jesus knew the man was greedy. The man wanted what his brother had. He wanted some of the money. He thought that he deserved the money. He was not happy with what he had. That is why he and his brother had an argument.

Jesus told the people to watch out for greed. (verse 15) Greed makes people want more and more money. Greed makes people want more things. Greed makes people unhappy with what they have. Greed can make us do wrong things and have wrong thoughts. Greed can cause us to sin.

Jesus did not say that money is bad. He knows that we must have money to buy food and clothes. We need money to buy what we need. He knows that we can help other people with money. We can

50

do many good things with money. But, Jesus knows that money can make us greedy.

B. JESUS SAID THAT WE SHOULD PLAN FOR ETERNITY.
    (Luke 12:16-21)

Jesus told the people a parable about a wealthy farmer. One year, he harvested a large crop. He harvested a larger crop than ever before. But he had no place to put the food. So, he decided to **destroy** his barns and build bigger barns. Then he would have a place for his crops.

The farmer said to himself, "Now, I have many good things. I have enough food for many years in the future. I can rest and enjoy life. I can eat, drink, and be happy."

God said that the man was foolish. God called the wealthy farmer a fool. God said that the man would die that very night. The man was not foolish because he was rich. He was not foolish because he harvested a large crop. He was foolish because he forgot God.

The farmer made three mistakes. First, he thought he would be happy if he owned many things. But, many things do not make us happy. Second, the farmer thought his crops would last for many years. He thought he could rest and enjoy life. But, crops may be destroyed by a fire or a storm. Third, the farmer thought he would live a long life. But, any person can die anytime.

The foolish farmer did not plan for eternity. He only planned for his life on earth. He did not think about his life after death. He was called a fool because he forgot God.

C. JESUS SAID THAT WE SHOULD WORK FOR THINGS THAT LAST
    FOREVER. (Matthew 6:19-21)

Jesus said, "Do not **store up** for yourselves treasures on earth . . ." (verse 19) We are greedy when we store up treasures for ourselves. We are thinking only of ourselves. We want to rest and enjoy life. But, our treasures can be destroyed. Fire may burn them up. Robbers may steal them. We are foolish to store up things here only for ourselves.

Instead, Jesus said to store up treasures in heaven. Jesus meant that our gifts to God will last forever. Our treasures in heaven are what we share with God and others. What we give to God cannot be burned or stolen. Our treasures in heaven cannot be destroyed. Our treasures in heaven will last for eternity.

The memory verse is important. Jesus knew that if we store up treasures in heaven we will not be greedy. We plan for eternity when we store up treasures in heaven. We plan for heaven because that is where our heart or thoughts are.

CONCLUSION

Today, each person should plan for eternity. We plan for heaven when we are not greedy. We plan for eternity when we remember God. We plan for eternity when we store up treasures in heaven.

QUESTIONS: *Fill in the blanks.*

1. _____ makes people want more and more money. Greed makes people unhappy with _____

   _____ _____ ,

2. Jesus did not say that _____ is bad. But money can make us _____.

3. Jesus told a _____ about a wealthy farmer. The farmer _____ a large crop. He decided to build

   _____ _____ .

4. God said the farmer was _____ because he

   _____.

5. The foolish farmer did not plan for _____.

6. Jesus said not to _____ _____ for ourselves _____ on earth.

7. We are to store up treasures in _____.

8. Our treasures in heaven are what we _____

   _____.

Here are some questions for you to think about and discuss:

1. How are people greedy today? Are you greedy?
2. Have you planned for eternity? How can people plan for eternity?
3. What are "treasures on earth?"
4. What are "treasures in heaven?" Do you have any treasures in heaven?

VOCABULARY:

1. **greed** (*noun*); **greedy** (*adjective*): wanting more and more things; not happy with what you own or have
2. **eternity** (*noun*): life after death; the future life of Christians in heaven; also the future life of sinners in hell
3. **argument** (*noun*): a fight with words; the talk when people do not agree with each other
4. **destroy** (*verb*): get rid of; make something so that it can no longer be used; put an end to
5. **store up** (*verb phrase*): put in a place for future use; save for the future

13 JESUS TAUGHT ABOUT BEING FAITHFUL

Memory Verse: ". . . Well done, good and faithful servant! You have been faithful . . ." (Matthew 25:21 and 23)
Scripture Lesson: Matthew 25:14-30

In this book, we have studied several teachings of Jesus. We have studied several of Jesus' parables. We have learned some important truths in these lessons.

In this last lesson, we will study one more parable. This story will help us learn about being faithful to God. This is also an important truth.

A. EVERY PERSON HAS A JOB TO DO. (Matthew 25:14-15)

Jesus told His disciples this story. One day, a man went on a trip. He asked three **servants** to take care of his things. He gave the first servant five **talents** of money. He gave the second servant two talents of money. He gave the third servant one talent of money. The man gave talents to each servant according to each one's **ability**. Each servant had a job to do.

In this story, a talent is an amount of money. Today, talent usually means ability. A talent is what a person does well. A talent may be the ability to sing or write. It may be the ability to work with your hands. It may be the ability to teach or preach.

God has given all of us one or more talents. God has given every person the ability to do certain things. All of us can do certain things well. God gives us talents according to our abilities.

Jesus told this story to help us understand that God is like the man. God gives us jobs to do. God **expects** us to do the jobs and do them well. He expects us to do the best we can. He expects us to use our talents for Him. He expects us to be faithful.

God does not expect every person to sing well. He does not expect every person to teach or preach. He does not expect all people to be good cooks. But God expects us to use our talents. Some people have more talents than others. But all Christians have at least one talent. Persons with one talent may think that they do not need to do much. They may think that they are not important. But their one talent is important. Their job is important to God. Therefore, they must be faithful in using their talent for God.

B. GOD REWARDS FAITHFUL WORKERS. (Matthew 25:16-23)

In the story, two of the servants used their talents wisely. They used their money to make more money. The man with five talents of money made five more talents. The man with two talents of money made two more talents. Their money made two times as much money as they had been given. These servants worked hard. They had been faithful.

Then, the man returned from his trip. He was pleased with these two servants. He knew that they did their jobs well. They were faithful servants. So he gave them a reward. He told them that he would let them care for many things. He would give them even bigger jobs.

Today, God trusts us with the jobs that He gives us. He trusts us with our talents. He expects us to be faithful. And He is pleased when we are faithful. He rewards us for doing a good job. He rewards us for being faithful.

C. GOD PUNISHES UNFAITHFUL WORKERS. (Matthew 25:24-30)

In the story, the servant with one talent hid his money. He hid the money in the ground. He did not do what the man asked him to do. He did not do what was expected. The servant was unfaithful.

The man was not pleased with this servant. He knew that the servant had not done his job. So, he punished the unfaithful servant. His talent of money was given to the faithful servants. The unfaithful servant was fired from his job. He had to leave the man's house.

Today, God expects us to be faithful. He expects us to do the best we can. But if we are not faithful, He will punish us. God will not reward unfaithful servants.

CONCLUSION

God gives talents or abilities to every person. He expects us to use our talents for Him. He expects us to be faithful. God will reward faithful servants. And He will punish unfaithful servants. We must decide what type of servants we will be.

If we are faithful, God is pleased. One day, He will say to us "Well done, good and faithful servant. You have been faithful." Every Christian wants to hear these words from our Lord. These are wonderful words. These words will be a part of our reward for being faithful.

QUESTIONS: *Give the answers.*

1. What did the man ask his servants to do? To take _____
   _____.

2. In this parable, what does "talent" mean? An amount of
   _____.

3. Today, what does "talent" mean? _____

4. What are two things that God expects of us?
   (a) _____
   (b) _____

5. Why were the two servants faithful? Because they used their
   money _____.

6. Why was the one servant unfaithful? Because he did not do what
   the man _____.

7. Whom does God reward? _____
   Whom does God punish? _____

8. What will God say to Christians if they are faithful?
   "... _____
   _____ ..."

   (Matthew 25:21 and 23)

Here are some questions for you to think about and discuss:

1. What talent or talents has God given to you?
2. How are you using your talent or talents for God?
3. Are you faithful? How can Christians be faithful? How can you be faithful?
4. What are the rewards Christians get for being faithful?

VOCABULARY:

1. **servant** (*noun*): a person who works for or serves another person;

56

(Today, a servant may be anyone who does a job for someone else.)

2. **talents** (*noun*): what people can do very well; anything a person does well, such as singing, playing the piano, doing artwork, cooking, speaking, and teaching

3. **ability** (*noun*): what a person can do; the skill or skills people have; (An ability may be a talent. It may also be something people have worked and trained themselves to do well.)

4. **expects** (*verb*): believes something should happen; thinks something is certain

INTRODUCTION FOR TEACHERS

The intercultural English lessons in this book have been developed for people who are developing proficiency in English. The intended audience includes bilingual speakers, such as new immigrants and ESL (English as a second language) learners, and English speakers who are preliterate and learning disabled. Also, new Christians and people with a limited knowledge of Bible truths can benefit by the simple, brief lessons. Such people can profit from materials with a controlled vocabulary and sentence structure to help them better understand the Bible and Christian concepts.

The target audience is the intermediate-level student who can work comfortably with a 2,200-word vocabulary. The writers, therefore, have been given careful consideration to both the vocabulary and sentence structure.

New words and phrases, ten items or less, have been introduced in each lesson. The words/phrases appear in the vocabulary list as they appear in the lesson text, both in form and sequence. The parts of speech have been included as an aid for teaching English.

In applying linguistic controls, the language has been simplified. The writers have purposely sacrificed style for simplicity in order to obtain English at a level that is more easily read and understood by the target audience.

The lessons, based on previously written Bible studies, have been adapted to **Intercultural English** to serve as transition materials while the learners are gaining Bible knowledge and English skills. The adaptation has also involved deleting content and language (such as illustrations, examples, poetry, figures of speech, etc.) that may be inappropriate in a cross-cultural learning situation.

There are three appendixes in this section, *Teacher Resources*. Appendix A contains suggested answers to the study questions. Appendix B includes all the vocabulary introduced in the lessons. Appendix C includes several useful tips for teaching. Teachers should become familiar with this supplementary information.

We believe this type of Bible study material meets a vital need which exists today in evangelical Christianity. We pray that God will honor His Word as it becomes a part of the learners' minds—**and hearts**—through the medium of **Intercultural English**.

Intercultural English Advisory Council
J. Wesley Eby, Chair

ANSWERS TO QUESTIONS

For each lesson there is a set of suggested answers for the study questions. You will find the intended answers, along with some possible alternatives or extensions (in parentheses), which are all correct in the context of the lessons. Teachers should be willing to accept any answer that can be justified.

Lesson 1
1. parables
2. kingdom of heaven
3. lessons
4. enjoy; remember
5. train
6. explained
7. share
8. treasures

Lesson 2
1. two (2)
2. part; wealth
3. all his money
4. go back home (ask his father to forgive him)
5. forgive him (forgave his son)
6. we are (us)
7. ask (for forgiveness)
8. loves us (very much)

Lesson 3
1. Christians; Word of God
2. plant the Word of God
3. four (4); soil
4. devil; Word of God
5. Jesus; problems; faith

6. choke; spiritual
7. harvest of people
8. listeners; obey

Lesson 4
1. 38; 16
2. was not honest (cheated)
3. God
4. think about our future (plan carefully; be honest)
5. trustworthy (with what we have)
6. use their money only for themselves (buy things we do not need; buy things that hurt themselves or other people; cheat other people)
7. to buy what they need (share with other people; for God's work)
8. good managers

Lesson 5
1. landowner; vineyard (grape farm)

2. hired (needed)
3. workers; job
4. deserved; worked
5. faithful
6. owe; Son; die; sins
7. we love Him
8. Lord; reward; good; Ephesians; 8

Lesson 6

1. God; our neighbors
2. Jerusalem; Jericho
3. Some robbers beat him. (The robbers took his clothes and money. He almost died. [Other answers are possible.])
4. priest; Levite
5. (good) Samaritan
6. (good) Samaritan
7. Christian love; (the love of Jesus or Jesus' love)
8. loved us so much that He died on a cross (died to save us from sin)

Lesson 7

1 . the Lord's prayer
2. persist
3. bold; afraid
4. ask; seek; knock
5. what we need
6. God's will
7. futures
8. Father; heaven; good gifts; best

Lesson 8

1. (a) Pharisee

2. wanted them to be humble (did not want people to think they were important)
3. least important
4. other people
5. Pharisee; tax collector
6. tax collector (humble man)
7. how good he was
8. exalted

Lesson 9

1. to love less
2. demand (command, tell); love
3. changes; think (live); do
4. carry his cross; follow; disciple
5. Jesus (God); obey (follow)
6. following; obeying
7. A. (Jesus demands) that we love Him more than anyone else.
   B. (Jesus demands) that we obey Him every day.
   C. (Jesus demands) that we plan carefully to be His disciple.

Lesson 10

1. seeds that grow (the [a] mustard seed)
2. we tell people about Jesus
3. words; actions
4. Paul (Apollos)
5. Apollos (Paul)
6. God
7. we are faithful

8. all of us (every person)

Lesson 11

1. Sermon on the Mount
2. Jesus; God; sorry; sins; forgive; received; lives
3. will; enter
4. wise builder; strong foundation (rock)
5. teachings; Jesus (Bible; God)
6. spiritual; safe
7. trusted
8. wise; foolish

Lesson 12

1. greed; what they have
2. money; greedy
3. parable; harvested; bigger barns
4. foolish (a fool); forgot God
5. eternity
6. store up; treasures
7. heaven

8. share with God and others

Lesson 13

1. care of his things (money; talents)
2. money
3. ability (what a person does well)
4. to do the jobs and do them well; to do the best we can; to use our talents for Him; to be faithful (Note: Any of these answers are correct.)
5. to make more money (wisely)
6. asked him to do
7. faithful workers (servants); unfaithful workers (servants)
8. ". . . Well done, good and faithful servant. You have been faithful . . ."

APPENDIX B
NEW VOCABULARY

Below is an alphabetical list of all the words and phrases in the Vocabulary sections in the lessons. The numbers following the definitions indicate the lessons where the words or phrases were introduced.

ability (*noun*): what a person can do; the skill or skills people have; (An ability may be a talent. It may also be something people have worked and trained themselves to do well.) [13]

actions (*noun*): deeds; acts; the things people do [6]

argument (*noun*): a fight with words; the talk when people do not agree with each other [12]

ashamed (*adjective*): felt shame or guilt; felt bad because you made a mistake or did something wrong [8]

bold (*adjective*): not afraid; brave; have no fear [7]

borrowing (*verb*): asking to use something that another person owns; (You agree to return what you borrow.) [7]

builder (*noun*): a person who builds [9]

carry his cross, carry a cross (*verb phrase*): obey Jesus completely; do God's will; follow Jesus and do what He says [9]

celebrated (*verb*): took part in a special time of joy; (Today, "celebrated" often is used in talking about parties and happy times, such as holidays.) [2]

cheating (*verb*): taking something by not being honest; stealing by tricking another person [4]

choke (*verb*): cause something to stop growing [3]

compared (*verb*): showed through words how things are alike [10]

custom (*noun*): a habit; something people do as a part of their way of living [2]

debtors (*noun*): people who owe something to other people [4]

decided (*verb*): chose; made a choice after thinking about it [2]

demands (*verb*): commands; says we should [9]

deserved (*verb*): earned; should be paid; were good enough for [5]

destroy (*verb*): get rid of; make something so that it can no longer be used; put an end to [12]

devil (*noun*): Satan; the enemy of God; the most powerful of evil spirits [3]

disciples (*noun*): the 12 men who followed Jesus here on earth and helped Jesus in His work [1]

discipleship (*noun*): being a disciple of Jesus; living the Christian life; obeying Jesus completely; doing God's will [9]

dishonest (*adjective*): not honest; not trustworthy [4]

divided (*verb*): made into two or more parts [2]

enter (*verb*): go or come into; become a part of [11]

eternal life (*noun phrase*): life that has no end; life as a child of God on earth and living with God in heaven forever [5]

eternity (*noun*): life after death; the future life of Christians in heaven; also the future life of sinners in hell [12]

exalted (*adjective*): made important; honored; gave praise to [8]

expects (*verb*): believes something should happen; thinks something is certain [13]

explain (*verb*): tell what something means; teach; tell all about something so other people will know about it too [1]

faithful (*adjective*): trustworthy; can be trusted; true to God; always does what should be done [5]

fired (*verb*): took a job away from someone; (People are fired when they are no longer wanted or needed for work.) [4]

foolish (*adjective*): not wise; (Foolish describes a person who does something without careful and wise planning.) [11]

forgiveness (*noun*): the act of forgiving someone; the act of God when he makes a person free from the guilt of sin [2]

foundation (*noun*): the base upon which a building or tower is built; (A strong foundation is needed so the building or tower will not fall down.) [9]

freedom (*noun*): the right to do what a person wants to do [2]

God's will (*noun phrase*): what God wants for people [7]

Gospels (*proper noun*): the first four books of the New Testament:

Matthew, Mark, Luke, and John; (The Gospels tell about the life of Jesus Christ.) [4]

greed (*noun*); **greedy** (*adjective*): wanting more and more things; not happy with what you own or have [12]

harvest (*noun*): a crop of food that is ready to eat; (A harvest of people is everyone who believes in God and receives Jesus as Savior.) [3]

hired (*verb*): gave a job to someone; asked a person to work and gave them money for their work [4]

host (*noun*): a person who takes care of guests in his home [8]

humble (*adjective*): describes a person who does not think he is better than he is; not thinking of yourself as important [8]

humbles (*verb*): does not think of himself as important or better than other people [8]

inn (*noun*): a place to stay at night for people who travel; a motel or hotel [6]

kingdom of God (*noun phrase*): all the people who believe in and receive Jesus as Savior, now and forever; (The kingdom of God is the same as the kingdom of heaven. See Lesson 1.) [10]

kingdom of heaven (*noun phrase*): the kingdom of God; (The kingdom of heaven includes all people who believe and obey God. The kingdom of heaven is not the same as heaven.) [1]

landowner (*noun*): a person who owns land; (In this lesson, the landowner was a farmer of grapes.) [5]

Levite (*proper noun*): a person in the family of priests for the Jews; a religious or church leader of the Jews [6]

listeners (*noun*): people who hear what is said; people who listen, understand, and obey the teachings of Jesus [3]

managers (*noun*): people who take care of things that someone else owns [4]

master (*noun*): owner; someone or something that has power over people [4]

mercy (*noun*): help that is given to people who cannot help themselves; (God gives mercy to sinners when He forgives them. Sinners deserve to be punished for their sins.) [8]

miracles (*noun*): things that only God can do; (Miracles show the great power of God.) [11]

mustard (*noun*): a garden plant that is used in cooking food; (The mustard plant has a very small seed.) [10]

neighbors (*noun*): people who live near each other; (In this lesson, neighbors include all people on earth.) [6]

obedience (*noun*): the act of obeying; doing what someone demands or commands; doing what you know is right to do [11]

parables (*noun*): short stories about everyday life that teach important lessons; (Jesus often used parables when He taught His disciples and people.) [1]

persist (*verb*): not stop; not quit; not give up [7]

Pharisee (*proper noun*): a religious leader of the Jews [8]

plant the Word of God (*verb phrase*): tell other people what the Bible says; try to help people understand the teachings of Jesus [3]

planting seeds (*verb phrase*): putting seeds in the ground so they will grow [1]

priest (*noun*): a religious or church leader of the Jews; a man who gave messages from God to the people [6]

proclaim (*verb*): preach; teach; tell; share; (In this lesson, proclaim means to preach, teach, tell, or share the good news of Jesus.) [10]

prophesy (*noun*): preach; proclaim the Word of God; give a message from God to people; tell what will happen in the future [11]

prophet (*noun*): a person who speaks for God; (A prophet gives a message from God to people.) [1]

respect (*verb*): think well of a person; think of a person as important [8]

rewards (*noun*): money or things you receive for doing something well; what you receive for doing something that is not a part of your job; special pay for doing a job [5]

reward (*verb*): to pay someone for doing a job [5]

Samaritans (*proper noun*): people who lived in the country of Samaria; (Samaritans lived near the Jews. The Jews and Samaritans were neighbors but they hated each other.) [6]

seek (*verb*): look for; ask for; try to find [7]

servant (*noun*): a person who works for or serves another person; (Today, a servant may be anyone who does a job for someone else.) [13]

share (*verb*): give away; give some of what you have to other people; tell what you know to other people [1]

spiritual (*adjective*): describes something of the Spirit of God or Holy Spirit [3]

spiritual seeds (*noun phrase*): words or actions that help other people know about God and His love [10]

store up (*verb phrase*): put in a place for future use; save for the future [12]

talents (*noun*): what people can do very well; anything a person does well, such as singing, playing the piano, doing art work, cooking, speaking, and teaching [13]

tax collector (*noun phrase*): a person who gets tax money from people for a country or a government; (A tax collector in Jesus' time often cheated people and got rich. They were not liked or respected by other people.) [8]

teaching, teachings (*noun*): what is taught; what a teacher helps other people to learn [1]

tower (*noun*): a tall building; a strong building [9]

train (*verb*): tell and show someone else how to do something; help people learn to do certain things [1]

treasures (*noun*): things people own and love very much; things people own that are very important to them [people] [1]

trick (*verb*): to fool; not be honest with [6]

trusted (*adjective*): believed in; (Trusted describes a person who always does what must be done or he is asked to do.) [4]

trustworthy (*adjective*): can be trusted; will always do what should be done or is asked to do [4]

vineyard (*noun*): a garden or farm of grape plants or vines; a place where a farmer grows grapes [5]

wealth (*noun*): riches and much money; all that a person owns [2]

APPENDIX C
TEACHING HELPS

A. **Plan carefully and prayerfully.** Anything important enough to do is important enough to plan to do. Unplanned teaching usually results in disorganized instruction, resulting in minimal learning. A familiar maxim says, "If I fail to plan, I plan to fail." Your students are worthy of your careful planning and sincere prayers. Commit your teaching and the learners to God. He will help you as you do your best.

B. **Be sensitive to the learners' needs.** Your students will probably be at different levels, both in their Bible knowledge and language skills. Your task, which is not an easy one, is to discover *where* the learners are in their English skills and in their understanding of the Christian faith.

   Be aware, also, that the learners' *felt needs* may be different from their *real needs*. But their *felt needs* usually must be met first before you are able to help them with their *real needs*. In your class, you may find the *felt need* is to learn to read while the *real need* is to learn about God. And while you strive to meet the perceived or *felt need*, never lose sight of the *real need*.

   There is no special method to help you make this discovery. You DO need to become a people-watcher, however. Look for any hints the students may give in their body language and in what they say. Also, become involved in the learners' lives, both in and out of class. This will help you become much more aware of their backgrounds, their culture, their experiences, and, thus, their needs, *felt and real*. God will be faithful as you commit this *discovery process* to Him.

C. **Determine your objective.** An objective is the purpose for teaching. Your objective or aim, as a Christian teacher, is twofold: Bible content and English language skills. Knowing *what* you are teaching, and *why*, will help you be more confident as a teacher or tutor. As a result, your instruction will be more effective. Therefore, become familiar with the lesson content and, if possible, the language skills needed by the learners.

D. **Focus on comprehension.** This is extremely important! If the learners do not understand, your instruction will be of limited value. Of course, every student will not fully understand everything you teach. But, as a teacher or tutor, try to have each student take away some learning from each session. How much the students understand and learn will vary from person to person. Yet, as a teacher or tutor, your task is to faithfully plant the seeds of God's Word. Then the Holy Spirit will help those seeds to grow and bear fruit in the minds and hearts of the learners.

Some strategies for aiding comprehension are:

1. *Use easy-to-understand Bibles*, such as:

   - *The Holy Bible, New Century Version.* Thomas Nelson, Inc., P.O. Box 141000, Nashville, TN 37214

   - *Contemporary English Version.* American Bible Society, 1865 Broadway, New York, NY 10023

   - *Good News Translation Bible.* American Bible Society, 1865 Broadway, New York, NY 10023

   - *Holy Bible: New Life Version.* Christian Literature International, P.O. Box 777, Canby, OR 97013

   If the students are not native speakers of English, have the students read the Scripture in their first language. This will certainly aid their understanding. Some sources of Bibles in various languages are:

   - The American Bible Society, 1865 Broadway, New York, NY 10023.
   - Multi-Language Media, P.O. Box 301, Ephrata, PA 17522.
   - International Bible Society, 1820 Jet Stream Drive, Colorado Springs, CO 80921
   - The Bible League, P.O. Box 28000, Chicago, IL 60628

2. *Use the students' first language also, if their native language is other than English.* This is ideal and will result in the greatest amount of learning. If an interpreter is available, or if you know the language, use both languages in your teaching. If possible, give the interpreter the material to be taught before the class session so he/she can become familiar with the lesson content.

3. *Take additional time to teach a lesson, as needed.* You can divide a lesson into two or more parts, according to the needs of the learners. *Remember:* You're teaching people, not materials. Materials are only tools by which you accomplish your objectives or aims.

4. *Tell the learners what you plan to teach as you begin a lesson.* Make the students aware of the lesson content at the beginning of the class. Then after you have taught, give a brief review. Thus, the lesson plan should include these three steps: (1) telling what you are going to teach, (2) teaching, and (3) telling what you have just taught.

5. *Use the questions in the lessons as a part of your teaching.* Questions are an important part of teaching. If time permits, use the questions as a part of the lessons. Or if time is limited, assign the questions for home study and discuss them during the next class session as review and reinforcement. Avoid grading the answers in such a way that the students have a sense of failure. (See Section E.) *Note:* If the questions

are an out-of-class assignment, be aware that other family members or friends may help answer the questions.

6. *Don't assume the learners can read the lessons on their own.* If the learners cannot read English, teach the lessons orally. Once the students seem to be reading independently, don't assume they understand what they are reading. Pronouncing the words does not necessarily mean they can read with comprehension. Use oral questions and discussion to help you determine how much they understand.

7. *Work with new and unknown words both before and during the lesson.* Develop vocabulary in meaningful activities, avoiding word lists. Many of the high-frequency words of English (such as *the, but, or, of, by, because*) have limited or no meaning by themselves. Also, many nouns and verbs have multiple meanings. Vocabulary has little value if there is no useful meanings for the learners. Always work with words in phrases or sentences that have meaning for your students. Make flash cards by writing the new word on the front, and write sentences with the word on the back. Also, be careful in the use of idioms, figures of speech, and slang expressions.

8. *Add your own examples and stories that are appropriate for the lessons.* Nonbiblical examples and stories are not included since such examples and stories are different from culture to culture. Yet, such stories or examples are very effective in the learning process. Just make certain the stories, examples, or illustrations are appropriate and meaningful for your learners.

9. *Use real objects, pictures, and other audiovisual aids, as much as possible.* Bulletin boards, charts, flash cards, cassette tapes, etc., will make the lessons more effective.

E. **Teach for success.** This begins, of course, with focusing on comprehension. If the learners understand, then you should expect success.

1. *Give sincere praise.* Help the students know they are learning. Reinforce their self-worth as individuals and as God's children, created in His image.

2. *Capitalize on the learners' strengths and their correct responses.* Minimize their weaknesses and mistakes.

3. *Assume every student WANTS to learn, CAN learn, and WILL learn.* Then teach according to this belief.

F. **Be a good language model.** This is essential since people are introduced to language by listening to it. This is true for all native and most non-native English speakers. As a language model, however, you do not have to be perfect. Discard any worries you may have. Just be yourself, and do the best you can. Try these practical ideas:

1. *Be natural.* Use spoken English as it is naturally used by native English speakers. Be careful not to talk down to the learners by using "baby talk."

2. *Talk slowly.* Most learners, especially second language learners, better understand language if spoken a little slower than used in normal speech. Yet, the speaker must maintain appropriate volume, rhythm, stress, and phrasing. Some teachers err by increasing volume as they slow down their speech. The increased volume is often misinterpreted by the learners.

3. *Be clear in pronunciation.* Pronounce words distinctly, making certain that you do not omit or slur final consonant sounds. Try to be clear and precise in your pronunciation while retaining naturalness.

   Don't expect adults or older youth who are learning English as a second language to speak it as native speakers. Research indicates that the learners will probably always speak it with an accent. *Remember:* The goal is for the learners to be able to communicate in English. They can accomplish this goal even if their pronunciation is not perfect.

4. *Model correct language.* This is an important technique, especially for correcting mistakes. You can show the correct response, language usage, or pronunciation simply by "doing it" yourself. Don't require the students to correct all their mistakes. For each lesson, focus on only one or two mistakes you would like the learners to correct and master. Pointing out too many errors at a time can be discouraging and embarrassing for the learners.

5. *Read aloud often.* You, as the teacher or tutor, can model good reading and oral language as you read aloud to the students. Research indicates this is a valuable technique. And as you read, be expressive and enthusiastic.

   Students need to hear you read the Scriptures frequently as well as the entire lesson. Read a Bible passage or the lesson aloud first before the learners ever see it. Then, read it a second time while they follow along with their eyes. This provides them with needed auditory (ear) and visual (eye) introduction to the lesson before they read it on their own.

EDITOR'S NOTE:

This information on teaching is extremely limited. Entire textbooks have been written on this subject. Space requirements, however, require that this supplementary material be brief. I pray, though, that what you have read will assist you as you minister to your students.

J. Wesley Eby